AF244138

THE WISDOM YOGA SUTRAS OF VASISHTA

~ THE KEY TO ABSOLUTE FREEDOM ~

Compiled by Lalita Devi

Blooming Lotus Press

Published by Blooming Lotus Press

© 2016 Lalita Devi (The pen name for Lily Goncalves, in acknowledgement, that all knowledge comes from the source; the Supreme Consciousness.)

ISBN 978-0-9918521-4-7

www.blooming-lotus-yoga.com

All parts of this book may be reproduced with permission in writing from the author.

Compiled from Swami Venkatesananda's translation of The Yoga Vasishta

Caring for Dharma Books

Dharma books contain the sacred teachings of the sages and have the power to show the way towards liberation. As such, they should be treated with respect and reverence. Please never place them directly on the floor, step over them, point your feet towards them or take them into bathrooms. They should be kept in a clean place and ideally be covered in fabric when transported. No other mundane objects should be placed on top of them. If it is necessary to one day dispose of them, it is best to give them away to a library, place them at a base of a tree in the forest, or immerse them in a lake, river, or the ocean, rather than throwing them in the trash. Thank you for your understanding, love, and care of this book.

Other Publications in the Vidya Collection

Pure Wisdom Book 1

Spiritual Quotes to Lead Your Way Home

- Lalita Devi

Pure Wisdom Book 2

Sacred Teachings from the Source

- Lalita Devi

Mala Magic

How to Use a Rudraksha Mala to Awaken Your Divinity

- Lalita Devi

The Way of Oneness

Essential Teachings of Vedanta to Discover Your Natural State

- Shri Ramananda Mayi

Awakening the Bliss of Being

Essential Teachings of Yoga on the Soul's Journey to Enlightenment

- Shri Ramananda Mayi

Becoming the Goddess

Essential Teachings of Tantra on How to Embody Your Divinity

- Shri Ramananda Mayi

Dedication

To the Guru, the Supreme Light of Knowledge, who dispels the darkness of ignorance in order to uncover our natural state of pure luminosity and peace. Endless love and gratitude to Shri Guru Vasishta, Amma Shri Karunamayi, Shri Ramana Maharshi, and Lord Shiva Dakshnamurthi whose limitless compassion and grace showers One and All. May we rest and abide in our True Nature of Absolute Oneness - Supreme Peace and Bliss.

Infinite Pranams to Thy Holy Lotus Feet,

Lalita Devi

Special Thanks

To my most Beloved One, Ramananda Mayi, who tirelessly devotes countless hours to the service of one and all, and who both inspired me and greatly contributed to the compilation of Shri Guru Vasishta's masterpiece, *The Yoga Vasishta* in condensed sutra form. And a very special thanks to my mother and father who I adore like anything, and who have taught me the divine virtues of unconditional love, humility, patience, gratitude, courage, and sincerity.

Om Namah Shivaya Gurave
Sat Chit Ananda Murtayai
Nishprapanchaya Shantaya
Niralambaya Tejase
Om Shantih Shantih Shantihi

We Invoke the Pure Consciousness
of the Inner Teacher
Who Manifests as the Bliss of Self Awareness
Who is the Eternal Peace Beyond Appearances and
Who Illuminates the Path to Freedom
May There Be Only Peace

Preface

    The Wisdom Yoga Sutras of Vasishta are a selection of the quintessential teachings of the timeless masterpiece, *The Yoga Vasishta* - in whose poetic and powerful verses the truth of Reality is revealed for all of those who are ready to receive its awakening.

    The original spiritual text, *The Yoga Vasishta*, is a collection of over 32,000 shlokas (verses) of the Great Maharishi Vasishta in his discourse to the young Lord Rama. Lord Rama, who is considered to be a reincarnation of Lord Vishnu, is at the brink of enlightenment, and all but needs the wise advice of his family preceptor or Guru, Sage Vasishta, to let the light of Self-knowledge shine forth. Lord Rama, and all of those who were present at the king's royal court, were spell-bound as Guru Vasishta expounded the teachings of the Absolute Supreme Consciousness to dispel the darkness of ignorance and dawn the light of Self-knowledge.

    The Yoga Vasishta is a masterpiece of perfect knowledge and prose delivered through stories, metaphors, and examples to illicit the direct experience of the True Self. This vast knowledge covers the frustrations and sufferings one faces in the darkness of ignorance and the necessary requirements needed to reach the light of knowledge; liberation or absolute freedom. This sacred text also reveals the essence of creation, existence and the dissolution of the world appearance, as well as the means to liberation, the importance of meditation, and the blissful state of enlightenment itself.

Although scholars debate about the date in which this monumental text was written, the Great Mahatmas, or enlightened beings, would say that not only is time non-existent in the absolute sense, but it is of a far greater scale than anyone can imagine, in the relative sense. In this way, although some scholars attribute this scripture to being written down by the Great Sage Valmiki, somewhere between the 11th and 14th century AD, the Great Saints would date the written work to be of many thousands of centuries beforehand, and the oral teachings of the Absolute Supreme Consciousness to be of time immemorial.

The Wisdom Yoga Sutras of Vasishta are drawn from *Vasishta's Yoga*- a translated version of *The Yoga Vasishta*, from Sanskrit into English by Swami Venkatesananda of the Divine Life Society, Rishikesh, India. I have taken the liberty to abridge certain passages and change some of the words of this translation to meet the minds of the modern world and offer a succinct extraction of these nectarine words. Where commentary was necessary to contextualize the brilliant sutra presented, a brief explanation was humbly offered in italics.

The Yoga Vasishta is a classical Advaita Vedanta (non-dual) text that removes all suffering and ignorance by elucidating the truth of Reality- there is Oneness only; pure bliss, peace, and joy. *The Yoga Vasishta* is also known as *MahaRamayana*, *Arsha Ramayana*, *Vasishta Ramayana*, *Yogavasishta-Ramayana*, and *Jnanavasishta*.

The Wisdom Yoga Sutras of Vasishta are keys to absolute freedom and peace and are an invaluable inspiration on the pathway home. These sutras themselves are enough to trigger an awakening and the direct experience of the Supreme Consciousness- our natural state. When the time has ripened, such sacred wisdom or jnana texts as *The Yoga Vasishta* will call out for you. If one truly and wholeheartedly yearns for the truth, so shall they be guided back to the source.

May the impeccable words of Truth within these sutras spark the light of pure knowledge and absolute peace.

Om Tat Sat

Contents

Contents

Introduction

The Wisdom Yoga Sutras of Vasishta are the quintessential teachings of the classical spiritual Vedanta (non-dual) text *The Yoga Vasishta*. It expounds the highest teachings of truth and existence, and as such is meant for mature spiritual seekers. If there is a deep yearning for truth, if there is a quest to know thy Self, and if the enquiry of "Who am I?" and "What is existence?" has become of foremost import, then the time has ripened for you to be exposed to the ultimate truth.

The teachings embedded within these sutras is not easy for the conditioned mind to accept, nor for one that is identified with the physical body and the world. These teachings require an open mind and heart, free from concepts and ideas of what is reality. The teachings are revolutionary. If the mind rejects or reacts to such words, or if there is too much doubt and confusion, then it is best to put down this text and wait for another time to present itself. All knowledge is nectar when received with an open sky-like mind and heart but conversely becomes poison when confounded by the deception of the "I-ness" of ego. When in doubt, we can wait until clarity prevails. Ultimately, we will always be guided home.

The boundless compassion of the Great Rishis or enlightened Sages has brought forward these nectarine words to lead us straight to the Heart of the Truth. As such, it is a wise idea to read a passage, or two or three, and reflect and meditate upon them daily. Until one has observed or witnessed the conditionings of the mind, one cannot imagine, nor grasp,

but can laugh lovingly, at the magnitude of unconscious living that most beings exist in throughout their daily lives. Only by continuously reading, reflecting, and meditating upon these teachings does one gain mastery over the mind.

The sutras have been categorized into various themes so that they can be easily assimilated with our pure intelligence. When one quote or sutra isn't quite enough to consolidate the truth, then there are a number of sutras of a similar principle that can help solidify it. These themes can help one apply the truth to the principles that are currently arising within one's life- such as facing death, difficult relationships or understanding the karmic unfolding of events. Or conversely, one can simply open a page within this text and reflect upon the truth, as it is eternal.

As Guru Vasishta exclaims, the Supreme Truth is not attained without persistent effort, and therefore this text, or any other text pertaining to the ultimate truth, must be studied and applied until the final conclusion has been reached. Only then, will all unfold effortlessly, without volition, as the spontaneous arising of what is.

The Ego

"All suffering surely revolves around egotism (it is the 'I' who suffers), and egotism is the sole cause of mental distress."

Here, Guru Vasishta refers to the 'ego', 'ego-sense' or 'I" as that which identifies with the physical body and its personality, as well as something separate from the Supreme Self. It is this very misidentification that is the root of all pain and suffering. Where there is Oneness, there is all; second to none, full, complete and absolute perfection.

"Egotism eclipses self-control, destroys virtue and dissipates equanimity. Non-egotism alone is truth."

"To the one who has risen above the ego-sense, the whole universe appears to be worth less than a blade of grass."

"To those whose mind has attained utter quiescence (stillness), their house itself is the forest. If the mind is at peace and if there is no ego-sense, even cities are as void. On the other hand, forests are like cities to those whose heart is full of desires."

"The abandonment of ego-sense is the cessation of ignorance; this and nothing else is liberation. Whether this world exists or does not exist, its apprehension or recognition by the mind leads to sorrow; its non-recognition is bliss."

"Desire for liberation interferes with the fullness of the Self; absence of such desire promotes bondage! Hence, constant awareness is to be preferred. The sole cause for bondage and liberation is the movement in consciousness. Awareness of this ends this movement. The ego-sense ceases the very moment one observes it, for it has no support any longer. Then who is bound by whom or who is liberated by whom?"

"Realize 'I am not that ego-sense' and rest in pure awareness."

The World Appearance

"In all the experiences of happiness and unhappiness, as also in all hallucinations and imagination, it is the mind that does everything and it is the mind that experiences all this: mind is man."

"The mind itself is the soul; the mind experiences what it itself has projected out of itself. By that, it is bound. It is the state of the mind that determines the nature of the reincarnation of the soul. What one intensely wishes for he obtains sooner or later. If the mind is impure, its effects are also impure; if it is pure, its products are pure too."

"Of course, there is no mind without restlessness; restlessness is the very nature of mind. It is the work of this restlessness of the mind based on the Infinite Consciousness that appears as this world, that indeed is the power of the mind."

"They who are confirmed in their conviction that the Infinite Consciousness alone exists is instantly freed from thoughts of pleasure and is therefore tranquil and self-controlled. The mind is by nature inert: it borrows intelligence from the Consciousness which it pursues in order to gain the ability to experience. The mind thus comes into contact with whatever has been brought into being by the power or energy of

Consciousness. Thus, the mind exists by the grace of Consciousness, as it were; and it entertains various thoughts on account of its perception of this universe."

"It is this mind alone which is the cause of all objects in the world; the three worlds exist because of the mind stuff. When the mind vanishes the worlds vanish too."

"In reality, neither the objective universe, nor the perceiving self, nor perception as such, nor void, nor inertness exists; only One is, Cosmic Consciousness. In this, it is the mind that conjures up the diversity, diverse actions and experiences, the notion of bondage and the desire for liberation."

Mental Conditioning

"Experience, thinking (entertaining notions, etc.), mental conditioning and imagination are meaningless and are productive only of psychological distress. All the sorrows and misfortunes of life are rooted in, and rest in, sense experience and thinking."

"Only when one severs the very root of the mind with the weapon of non-conceptualization, can one reach the Absolute Brahman (Self) which is omnipresent, supreme peace. Conceptualization or imagination is productive of error and sorrow."

"Consciousness minus conceptualization is the eternal Brahman the Absolute; consciousness plus conceptualization is thought."

"Belief in the existence of the goblin creates it. Belief in duality (diversity) establishes it. When the nondual being is known, the duality vanishes instantly. Belief (or imagination) gives rise to diversity; when that belief is dropped, diversity goes. Thought, imagination or belief gives rise to sorrow; to abandon such thinking is not painful! It is feeding these thoughts and beliefs that has brought about this sorrow; and this comes to an end

by not entertaining those thoughts and beliefs: where is the difficulty in this? All thoughts and beliefs lead to sorrow, whereas no thought and no belief are pure bliss. Therefore, with the help of the fire of wisdom, vaporize the waters of your beliefs and become peaceful, supremely blissful. Behold the One Infinite Consciousness."

"After having firmly abandoned all contact with external objects turn the mind within and reflect over everything within yourself, even while engaged in various activities. With the help of this sharp sword of wisdom, cut through this network of conditioning (which throws up cravings, intentions, motivations, acceptance, and rejection) which alone is the cause of this stream of world appearance."

"If you remain unattached to them, unconcerned about them and without identifying yourself with them, through the strength of your consciousness or awareness these mental conditionings are greatly weakened."

"Notions and ideas gradually cease to arise and to expand in one who resolutely refrains from associating words with meanings, in his own mind—whether these words are uttered by others or they arise in one's own mind."

"First destroy the mental conditioning by renouncing cravings; and then remove from your mind even the concepts of bondage and liberation. Be totally free of conditioning. "

Here, Guru Vasishta equates mental conditioning, the conditioned mind, thoughts, imagination, desires, and concepts as bondage and the cause of all suffering. They are one in the same as the mind and the ego. The eradication of all thoughts, ideas, concepts, and conditioning is liberation- the state of 'no-mind'.

The Mind/Matter Connection

"A person is made of whatever is firmly established as the truth of their being in their own mind: that they are, naught else."

"The mind alone is the creator of the world.... What is done by the mind is action, what is done by the body is not action."

Here, Guru Vasishta is referring to the mind as all that is experienced as creation; as all that appears as the world. The world is an appearance made up of thought forms. Therefore, what is done, is the responsibility of the mind or thoughts. What is done by the body is governed by the mind, the mind is the sole creator and 'doer' of actions, within the world appearance.

"Mental and physical illness, as well as negative projections do not touch the mind that is devoted to the Self. Whatever the mind contemplates that instantly materializes. By intense contemplation it can bring about radical change within itself, to heal itself of the defective vision in which illusions were perceived as real. What the mind does, that it experiences as truth."

Guru Vasishta had previously mentioned that the ability to manifest through thought forms were the direct result of the degree to which the mind is pure. That is, a pure mind will manifest a thought instantly, whereas an impure mind may take a long while to manifest its thoughts. This is to be kept in mind in the above quote. The main essence of the above quote is centered around the ability of the mind to instantly dis-identify with the world illusion and therefore be free of pain and suffering. One who is dedicated to the Self is untouched by illness, projections or calamities of the outside world- they are merely a witness to it all.

"Whatever the mind seeks to attain, that the senses strive for with all their energy."

No-Mind

"When one's awareness is raised to one's Heart and firmly set in the Pure Consciousness, the mind naturally and effortlessly becomes tranquil... When thus the awareness of the Self becomes aware of the experience, then the experience does not leave an impression or memory on consciousness and is immediately 'forgotten', as it were. Even an attempt to do this takes one closer to the supreme state of Self-knowledge."

"One's mind is at rest who enjoys observing or watching oneself and is disinterested in external events and observations. When one's awareness is thus firmly held within oneself, the mind abandons its usual restlessness and flows towards wisdom."

"Whatever one does with a pure and clear mind which rests in equanimity, is right and appropriate, never defective."

"Attachment is that which makes the conditioning of the mind more and more dense, by repeatedly causing the experiences of pleasure and pain in relation to the existence and the nonexistence of the objects of pleasure. If you abandon this attachment which causes disturbances in you, the actions that you may spontaneously perform here will not affect you. If you

rise beyond joy and sorrow and therefore treat them alike, and if you are free from attraction, aversion, and fear, you are unattached. If you are independent of your own desires and hopes, and if you do not abandon your awareness of the homogeneity of the truth, you are unattached. If endowed with equal vision, you engage yourself in spontaneous and appropriate action in the here and now, you are unattached."

"They in whom the twin urges of acquisition and rejection have come to an end, do not desire anything nor do they renounce anything. The mind does not reach the state of utter tranquility till these two impulses (of acquisition and of rejection) have been eliminated. Even so, as long as one feels 'this is real' and 'this is unreal' the mind does not experience peace and equilibrium. How can equanimity, purity or dispassion arise in the mind of one who is swayed by thoughts of 'this is right', 'this is wrong' 'this is gain', 'this is loss'? When there is only the One Supreme Consciousness (which is forever one and the many) what can be said to be right and what wrong? As long as the mind is swayed by thoughts of the desirable and the undesirable there cannot be equanimity."

"It is not possible to 'kill the mind' without these methods:

1. knowledge of the Self
2. The company of awakened sages
3. the abandonment of conditioning
4. the restraint of the life-force (prana)

These are the means to overcome the mind. Ignoring these and resorting to violent practices like Hatha Yoga, austerities,

pilgrimage, rites, and rituals are a waste of time. Self-knowledge alone bestows delight on you.”

“Those who have attained inner tranquility and peace finds peace and tranquility everywhere in the world. Those whose mind is agitated and restless find the world full of restlessness. For, what one experiences within, that alone they experience outside. In fact, the sky, the earth, the air and the space, the mountains and the rivers are all parts of the inner instrument (the mind); they only appear to be outside. All these exist like the tree in the seed and they are externalized like the scent of a flower. Truly, there is nothing either inside or outside: whatever the Consciousness conceives of, in whatever manner, appears so. Thus the Self alone is all this, within and without.”

“Bondage is none other than the notion of an object, abandon the notions of 'I' and 'this' and remain established in the truth.”

Desire

"It is desire that is ignorance or mental conditioning: and the coming to an end of desire is liberation. This happens when there is no movement of thought in the mind. Wise words are mere words (ignorance) and not wisdom unless they are substantiated by the absence of desire and anger."

"There is a terrible elephant roaming in a forest working havoc. Desire is that elephant. It roams in the forest known as the body. It is maddened by sensuousness. It is restless with mental conditioning and thoughts. This elephant destroys everybody in this world. It is known by different names— desire, mental conditioning, mind, thought, feeling, attachment, etc. It should be slain by the weapon known as courage or determination born of the realization of Oneness."

"Only as long as one believes in objective existence does desire arise! This alone is samsara (the cycles of birth and death): the feeling 'This is'. It's cessation is liberation. This is the essence of wisdom. Recognition of 'objects' gives rise to desire. Non-recognition of objects ends desire. When desire ends, the soul drops its self-limitation. One is great who therefore abandons all thoughts concerning what has been experienced and what has not been experienced. I declare with uplifted arms that the thought-free, notion-less state is the best. Non-thinking is known as yoga. As long as thoughts of 'I'

and 'mine' persist, sorrow does not cease. When such thoughts
cease, sorrow ceases."

"They who rest in what is indicated by the 'All', 'Infinite' or
'Fullness', does not desire anything."

Death and Relationships

"All beings are your relatives, for in this universe there does not exist absolute un-relatedness. The wise know that 'There is nowhere where I am not': thus they overcome limitation or conditioning."

"You have had countless fathers and mothers. They have had countless children. Countless have been your incarnations! And, if you wish to grieve over the death of parents, why do you not grieve for all those countless beings unceasingly?"

"These false notions of father, mother, friend, relative, etc., are swept aside by wisdom as dust is swept away by the wind. These relatives are not based on truth, they are but words! If one is thought of as a friend, he is a friend; if he is thought of as the other, he is the other! When all this is seen as the One omnipresent being, where is the distinction between the friend and the other?"

"One who knows the deathless nature of the Self is not afraid of death. Nor are they affected by separation from friends and relations. The feelings 'This is I' and 'This is mine' are the mind; when they are removed, the mind ceases to be. Then one becomes fearless. Weapons like swords generate fear; the

weapon (wisdom) that destroys egotism generates fearlessness."

Existence

"Memory arises only in relation to the objective universe, thus providing the cause and effect sequence. The natural movement that arises in consciousness is also known as memory. When that movement occurs repeatedly it is seen externally as matter. When a thing is experienced by the consciousness even just a little and when that experience is repeated, a mental impression is created. Thus is the world appearance created."

"This world appearance is extremely subtle and it is built merely by mental activity or the movement of thought: it is like scent in the air. However, unlike such scent in the air, this world appearance is experienced only by the mind that conceives it, whereas scent can be experienced by others also. Just as one's dream is experienced only by the dreamer, this creation is experienced only by the one in whose mind it arises."

"The movement of energy that occurs in the Infinite Consciousness is known as the cosmic person who is endowed with a magnetic field and gravitational force. This creation arises in one like a dream. Creation is a dream. The waking state is a dream. Even though this creation or world appearance is apparently seen and experienced, it is, in reality, the realization of the notions that arise in us, and they alone

exist as the cosmic personality. Consciousness itself experiences the notions that arise in it again and again. It is that cosmic person who is pervaded and permeated by consciousness that appears as all the dream objects. Just as an actor who dreams that they are acting sees themselves acting on a stage entertaining an audience, this consciousness becomes aware of its own experience of this world appearance."

"As long as one experiences the perceived object as something real and substantial, this world appearance continues to flow."

"In every atom of existence, there are countless world appearances. Within every atom is the potential experience of every kind."

"Countless have been the universes that have come into being and that have been dissolved. In fact, even the countless universes that exist at this moment are impossible to conceive of. All this can immediately be realized in one's own Heart, for these universes are the creation of the desires that arise in the Heart, like castles built in the air. The individual conjures up this world in his Heart and while he is alive he strengthens this illusion; when they pass away they conjure up the world beyond and experiences it— thus there arise worlds within worlds just as there are layers within layers in a plantain stem."

Karma As Action

"You are not impelled to action by anything other than yourself. Hence you are free to strengthen the pure mental conditionings or tendencies in preference to the impure ones. The impure ones have to be abandoned gradually and the mind turned away from them little by little, lest there should be a violent reaction. By encouraging the pure tendencies to act repeatedly, strengthen them. The impure ones will weaken by disuse. When thus you have overcome the force of the impure tendencies then you will have to abandon even the good ones. You will then experience the Supreme Truth with the intelligence that rises from pure tendencies."

Here Guru Vasishta is explaining that Karma is action that arises from our thoughts or impressions, also called mental conditionings or tendencies. These conditionings come from past actions, of this birth or previous births, and can be of a pure or good nature, or of an impure or bad nature. The pure actions or good karma lead to a dharmic or righteous life, which ultimately leads one to the truth of Reality. Guru Vasishta further clarifies that all action, including pure or good karma, will eventually need to be abandoned in order to rest in our natural state which is Oneness only- without attributes of good or bad. This process of letting go of bad or impure tendencies and strengthening goods or pure ones, and finally letting go of being the doer of all actions (pure or impure), is a gradual process that needs to be employed with compassion and gentleness in order for the mind to remain peaceful and non-reactive.

"I feel that fate is nothing but the culmination of one's own action. Such is the course of action: action is non-different from the most potent among mental conditionings or tendencies, and these tendencies are non-different from the mind and the man is non-different from the mind!"

Guru Vasishta is emphasizing once again that all we experience, think, act and feel is nothing but the mind. Each person is essentially made up of whatever the mind conceives of at that moment. Fate or destiny is none other than the accumulation of past actions that must be played out, much like an arrow completing its course of action after being shot.

The Power of Manifestation

"People in whom the perception of division has been deep rooted do not have the power to realize their wish; when one like the Sage has weakened the perception of division it is possible for one to realize their wish."

"That mind is pure in which all cravings are in a state of quiescence (stillness). Whatever that pure mind wishes, that materializes."

Guru Vasishta is outlining the power of manifestation- that is, to the degree to which the mind is pure, will its capacity to manifest shine forth. An impure mind that is stuck in the delusion of division, that is taking the world appearance to be the ultimate Reality, will not have the capacity to manifest one's thoughts. The pure Sage-like mind, which is non-dual in essence, can manifest their wishes at will, instantaneously.

Karma As The Supreme Self

"What will be will be. Realize this truth."

"The will of the Supreme Being cannot be transgressed: it is its will that I should be like this and that the others should be as they are. One cannot fathom nor measure what has to be. In accordance with the nature of each being, that which is to be, comes to be."

"The cosmic order that people refer to as fate, divine will or destiny, and which ensures that every effort is blessed with appropriate fruition, is based on omnipresent and omnipotent omniscience, also known as the Supreme Self."

Guru Vasishta is now introducing the connection that karma, which is none other than past thought forms or mental conditionings is ultimately the Supreme Self. In this case, Guru Vasishta is equating the Supreme Being as the Supreme Self or the Supreme Consciousness, in which all that is referred to as destiny, divine will, or karma is ultimately none other than the Supreme Consciousness or the Supreme Being. In this way, Guru Vasishta is emphasizing that karma- that is the fruit of action- which is fixed or inevitable, must take its course of action due to past deeds, each for each individual. This explains why someone who is very

noble and saintly in this lifetime can have so many difficulties and disturbances come to them, seemingly undeservedly. It is very common in this case to feel as though "they don't deserve this" or feel "how unjust or unfair are these circumstances". It is true that the individual may be so pure and saintly in this lifetime but unfortunately needs to live out the repercussions of some of the impure deeds of past lives in this very lifetime.

The following excerpt comes from a story within The Yoga Vasishta whereby Vasishta is re-telling a conversation that a hunter had with a wise Sage of yore, in order to help clarify Vasishta's teaching on the inevitability of fixed karma:

The Hunter asked: Is there a means by which fate can be averted?

The Sage replied: That which is inevitable cannot be averted by anyone at any time. It is not altered by any amount of effort. The right arm is the right arm and the left arm is the left arm; no one can alter that fact. The head and the feet cannot be exchanged for one another. Whatever is, is. Even the science of astrology can only foretell what is to come, but it cannot avert what is bound inevitably to happen. However, the Sages of Self-knowledge live in this world as if in deep sleep. They experience the result of past actions without allowing the inner consciousness ever to become disturbed. They overcome all karmas.

"When people speak of God they imply what is inevitable, what is beyond their control and the events of natural order. Divine grace, natural order, and right self-exertion, all of them

refer to the same truth; the distinction is due to wrong perception or illusion."

Guru Vasishta is once again emphasizing that all is the Supreme Consciousness: God, Divine grace, destiny, karma, fate, the natural order of events, and right self-exertion (acting spontaneously without volition). The ultimate truth always comes back to Oneness only, creating a distinction between these, is failing to recognize this truth.

"Abandon the concept of diversity even while being engaged in diverse actions. You are not the doer of actions. One is regarded as a wise Sage whose actions are burnt in the fire of Self-knowledge and are therefore free from desire."

This is a fundamental teaching of karma: you are not the doer of your actions. That is, there is Oneness only; the Supreme Consciousness- all that is done is done through and by it only. To identify one's self as a separate individual who acts in the world independently is a major obstacle to Self-Realization. One who uses the fire of Self-knowledge and observes or witnesses all actions as though in a dream-like state, resting in the Supreme Consciousness, is free from doer-ship and therefore free from desires. Such is the state of liberation or absolute freedom.

The Necessity of Self-Effort

"The supreme state is not attained without effort."

"There is no power greater than right action in the present. One should never yield to laziness but strive to attain liberation, seeing that life is ebbing away every moment."

"Self-effort is of two categories: that of past births and that of this birth. The latter effectively counteracts the former. Fate is none other than self-effort of a past incarnation. There is constant conflict between these two in this incarnation; and that which is more powerful triumphs."

"Self-effort is based on these three—knowledge of scriptures, instructions of the teacher (guru) and one's own effort.... Hence, he who desires salvation should divert the impure mind to pure endeavor by persistent effort —this is the very essence of all scriptures."

"Self-effort is the mental, verbal and physical actions which are in accordance with the instructions of a holy person well versed in the scriptures."

"This much is certain: until one attains Self-knowledge, there is a need to strive for liberation. One should cultivate firm meditation. The means to this are (1) scriptures, (2) company of holy ones and (3) meditation. The ignorant sees the world as a physical reality, the wise as Consciousness. To the wise, there is neither ego sense nor the world. Their vision of the world is indescribably wonderful."

Spiritual Practice

"The very best intelligent means by which the mind can be subdued is complete freedom from desire, hope or expectation in regard to all objects at all times. It is very difficult for one who does not engage themselves in serious practice, but very easy for one who is earnest in their effort. There is no harvest without sowing: the mind is not subdued without persistent practice."

"Adhering to the teachings of the scriptures one should patiently wait for perfection which comes in its own time. Arrest the downward trend by studying this holy scripture for liberation. Enquire constantly into the nature of truth, knowing that 'this is but a reflection'."

"Reject the reality of the mind from a great distance and be ever devoted to right thinking and meditation."

"Determined and persistent self-effort is considered the best: in its absence, other forms of worship are prescribed."

"Strive by every means to remain vigilant in Self-knowledge. When you do not engage yourself in sense experiences and

also when you experience whatever comes to you unsought, you are in a state of equanimity and purity, free from mental conditionings or memories. In such a state, like the sky, you will not be tainted even by a thousand distractions."

"True, all these beings are real to one another. To the extent they perceive one another they experience one another. You have heard all this, but you do not rest in the truth. Only by constant practice does this truth become fully established."

"When this mind confidently engages in self-effort, then it is beyond the reach of sorrow."

The Relationship Between Mind and Prana

"Movement of thought in the mind arises from the movement of prana (life-force), and movement of prana arises because of the movement of thought in consciousness."

"Mind and the movement of thought are inseparable; and the cessation of one is the cessation of both. There are two ways in which this cessation can be achieved: one is the way of yoga which involves the restraint of the movement of thought, and the other is the way of knowledge which involves the right knowledge of truth."

"Of the two seeds for this world illusion- that is the movement of prana or the clinging to thoughts- if one is got rid of the other also goes away; for the two are interdependent. The mind creates the world illusion and the mind is created by the movement of prana in one's own conditioning. Again, this movement of prana also takes place because of the mental conditioning or thoughts. Thus this vicious circle is completed; one feeds the other, one spurs the other into action. Motion is natural to prana and when it moves in consciousness, mind arises; then the mental conditioning keeps the prana in motion. When one is arrested, both fall."

"Wise ones declare that the abandonment of mental conditioning (thoughts) and the restraint of prana are of equal effect: hence, one should practice them simultaneously. Prana is restrained by the practice of pranayama (restraint of the movement of prana) and by yoga asana, as taught by the guru, or by other means."

"By the devoted and dedicated practice of either the cessation of the movement of prana or the cessation of thought, liberation is attained. This is the essence of all scriptures dealing with liberation."

"The wise ones declare that the mind is caused by the movement of prana; and hence by the restraint of the prana, the mind becomes quiescent (still). When the mind abandons the movement of thought, the appearance of the world illusion ceases."

Pranayama

"In order to bring about the stillness of the mind, the yogi practices pranayama (restraint of the movement of the life-force), meditation and such other proper and appropriate methods. Great yogis regard this pranayama itself as the most appropriate method for the achievement of tranquility of the mind, peace, etc."

"Without considerations of being or nonbeing, desirable and undesirable, I remain in the Self: hence I am happy, healthy and free from illness because I contemplate the moment of union of the prana (inhale) and the apana (exhale) when the Self is revealed."

Guru Vasishta is describing two of the vital airs called "prana" and "apana". Whereas the word prana is used to describe one's subtle energy field called the life-force, it is also the name given to one of the 5 vital airs which are a categorization of one's subtle energy field at large. Prana is in this case equated with the in-breath or inhale, and apana with the out-breath or exhale. When these two vital airs meet- that is after inhaling and before exhaling, or after exhaling and before inhaling, there is a gap. This gap is pure stillness and is our natural state. It is where the Self is revealed.

"The life-force is restrained by the following means:

1. Dispassion (non-attachment and non-aversion)
2. Pranayama (restraint of life-force)
3. Enquiry into the cause of the movement of the life-force (Self-enauiry)
4. By the ending of sorrow through intelligent means (Self-knowledge through wisdom and discernment, the study of the truth - sacred texts, instructions from the Guru, and Self-effort)
5. Direct knowledge or experience of the Supreme Truth"

The Conditioned Mind

"Total dedication to one thing, the restraint of prana, and the cessation of the mind—if one of these three is perfected, one attains the Supreme State. The life-force and the mind are closely related like a flower and its fragrance, or sesame seed and oil. Hence, if the movement of thought in the mind ceases, the movement of prana ceases, too. If the total mind is one pointedly devoted to a single truth, the movement of the mind and therefore of the life-force ceases. The best method is by enquiring into the nature of the Self which is infinite. Your mind will be completely absorbed. Then both the mind and the enquiry will cease. Remain firmly established in what remains after that."

"The notion of an object (of knowledge, of experience) is the seed for both the movement of prana and for the clinging to thought, for it is only when such desire for experience arises in the Heart that such movement of prana and mental conditioning takes place. When such desire for experience is abandoned, both these cease instantly...... strive to eradicate the desire for experience. Free yourself from all experiences."

"He who has no desire or hope for anything here, nor entertains a wish to rest in inactivity. He who does not lean towards experience or perception of objects, though he is engaged in ceaseless activity, he is neither inactive nor does he do anything or experience anything. The objective experiences do not touch the Heart at all. Freed from all conditioning, fully established in the state of unmodified consciousness, the yogi remains like a child or a dumb person: in him, there is bliss, like the blueness of the sky. This bliss is not an experience, but the very nature of Consciousness."

The Four Gatekeepers to Liberation

"There are 4 gatekeepers at the entrance to the Realm of Freedom (Liberation). They are Self-control, Self-enquiry, Contentment, and Satsanga. The wise seeker should diligently cultivate the friendship of these or at least one of them."

1. SELF-CONTROL

"When the mind is at peace, pure, tranquil, free from delusion or hallucination, untangled and free from cravings, it does not long for anything nor does it reject anything. This is self-control or conquest of the mind."

"One who looks upon all beings with equal vision, having brought under control the sensations of pleasure and pain, is self-controlled. One who, though living amongst all is unaffected by them, neither feels elated nor hates, even as one is during sleep—is self-controlled."

2. SELF-ENQUIRY

"Enquiry should be undertaken by an intelligence that has been purified by a close study of the scriptures, and this enquiry should be unbroken. By such enquiry the intelligence becomes keen and is able to realize the Supreme; hence enquiry alone is the best remedy for the long lasting illness known as samsara (cycles of birth and death)."

3. CONTENTMENT

"To renounce all craving for what is not obtained unsought and to be satisfied with what comes unsought, without being elated or depressed even by them—this is contentment. With the rise of contentment the purity of one's heart blooms. The contented one who possesses nothing owns the world."

4. SATSANGA
(the company of wise, holy and enlightened people)

"Satsanga enlarges one's intelligence, destroys one's ignorance, and psychological distress. Whatever be the cost, however difficult it may be, whatever obstacles may stand in its way, satsanga should never be neglected. For, satsanga alone is one's light on the path of life."

"Satsanga is indeed superior to all other forms of religious practice like charity, austerity, pilgrimage and the performance of religious rites."

"One should by every means in one's power adore and serve the holy saints who have realized the truth and in whose Heart the darkness of ignorance has been dispelled. They who, on the other hand, treat such holy saints disrespectfully, surely invite great suffering."

"One who enjoys the company of enlightened ones does not suffer in this world, even as one who holds a candle in his hand does not see darkness anywhere."

"It is only when the Self is seen that the highest form of dispassion (non-attachment and non-aversion) becomes firmly rooted in the Heart. Hence, one should simultaneously behold the Self through intelligent enquiry, and thereby get rid of the craving for pleasure. When the intelligence is still un-awakened, one should fill two quarters of the mind with the enjoyment of pleasure, one part with the study of scriptures and the other with service to the Guru. When it is partially awakened, two parts are given over to the service of the Guru and the others get one part each. When it is fully awakened, two parts are devoted to service of the Guru and the other two to the study of scriptures, with dispassion as the constant companion."

The Guru

"This ocean of samsara (cycles of birth and death) is impassable except with the help of the saints. One should not become passive, fatalistically accepting whatever happens. Hence, one should abandon all other activities and be devoted to the saintly ones. This alone is capable of bestowing on one the best of both the worlds. One should never be far away from the saints, for by their very proximity the saints promote goodness everywhere."

"By the practice of the teachings of the scriptures, the mind becomes pure and transparent; then without even wishing for it one sees the Supreme Truth. The scriptures promote the sattvic (pure) part of ignorance, which gives purity of mind. This purity destroys the tamasic (dull) part of ignorance. Hence, the Supreme Truth is realized when one contemplates the real meaning of the scriptures with the aid of the words of the Guru, the satsanga (the company of saints), self-discipline and the control of the mind."

Spiritual Knowledge

"This much is certain: until one attains Self-knowledge, there is a need to strive for liberation. One should cultivate firm meditation. The means to this are (1) scriptures, (2) company of saints and (3) meditation. The ignorant sees the world as a physical reality, the wise as Consciousness. To the wise, there is neither ego-sense nor the world. His vision of the world is indescribably wonderful."

"Being and nonbeing (like prosperity and adversity) when they follow each other creating diverse and even great contradictions, do not generate joy and sorrow in the holy saints. The means for crossing this ocean of samsara (cycles of birth and death) and for the attainment of Supreme peace are an enquiry into the nature of the Self (Who am I?) and of the world (What is this world?) and of the truth (What is truth?)."

"The thinking that is brought about by hopes and cravings is known as 'vrtti' (movement of thought); when hopes and cravings are given up, there are no vrtti either. When the mind is free from movements of thought (which are motivated by hopes or cravings) then it becomes no-mind: and that is liberation."

"In order to reach the state of perfection or liberation taught by me, you should live a life of non-attachment, doing what is appropriate in every situation as it reaches you. Rest assured that this is the vital factor in the teachings of all scriptures."

"Remain unattached, endowed with the spirit of renunciation and with the realization that whatever you do or you experience is an offering to the omnipresent being, the Supreme Self. Then you will realize the truth, and that is the end of all doubts."

"The Sages perceive the middle path, they see what is at the moment, they are at peace, they are established in the witness consciousness."

"Knowledge does not have an object to know. Knowledge is independent and eternal; it is beyond description and definition. When this truth is directly realized there is perfect knowledge."

"This is the supreme meditation, this is the supreme worship: the continuous and unbroken awareness of the indwelling presence, inner light or Consciousness. While doing whatever one is doing—seeing, hearing, touching, smelling, eating, moving, sleeping, breathing or talking—one should realize one's essential nature as pure Consciousness. Thus does one attain liberation."

Self-Realization

"Resort to the understanding of non-duality, for the truth is nondual; however, action involves duality and hence functions in apparent duality—thus, let your nature partake of both duality and non-duality."

"Live in the present, with your consciousness externalized momentarily but without any effort: when the mind stops linking itself to the past and to the future, it becomes no-mind. If from moment to moment your mind dwells on what is and drops it effortlessly at once, the mind becomes no-mind, full of purity."

"That is samadhi (contemplation or meditation) in which one realizes the objects of the senses as not Self, and thus one enjoys inner calmness and tranquility at all times. The non-action of the mind is known as quiescence (stillness); it is total freedom, it is blessedness."

"The Sage, knowing that beings are constantly born and that they die constantly, does not give way to joy or grief. They know that the world arises in their own vision, even as the dream objects arise when one dreams, and hence all these objects are of momentary existence. Therefore, they do not

feel any justification for either pity or joy. When all such concepts like pleasure and pain, desirable and undesirable cease, all notions in the mind cease."

"They who see the Self as the transcendent being or as the immanent being (as the Self of all) is established in equanimity. They in whom likes and dislikes have ceased, to whom all beings are the same and who perceives the world in the wakeful state as if they perceive objects in a dream, they are established in equanimity and view a city or a village as a forest."

"No delight in the world is comparable to the delight that will fill your Heart when you completely abandon all desires and hopes. Not in kingship, nor in heaven, nor in the company of the beloved one does one experience such delight as when one is free from hope."

When Guru Vasishta speaks about abandoning all desires, which include hope, He is speaking about the need to let go of all expectations, including the hope for something to occur, or not to occur. In this way, hope itself becomes bondage when our expectations are not met, and further thought forms such as disappointment or dissatisfaction result in its wake. This suggestion to abandon all hope is for a mature spiritual seeker that is able to meet each moment as it arises without attachment or aversion. For those new to the spiritual path, it is wise to encourage one to foster hope in order to strengthen one's pure tendencies over the impure ones- thereby gaining the necessary

knowledge and direct experience to be able to let go of all hoping in the future.

"It is only when the mind has become devoid of all attachment, when it is not swayed by the pairs of opposites, when it is not attracted by objects and when it is totally independent of all supports, that it is freed from the cage of delusion. When all doubt comes to rest and when there is neither elation nor depression, then the mind shines like the full moon. When the impurities of the mind have ceased to be, there arise in the Heart all the auspicious qualities, and there is equal vision everywhere."

"The difference between contemplation and its absence is indicated by whether or not there is movement of thought in the mind: hence make the mind unconditioned. The unconditioned mind is firm, and that in itself is meditation, freedom, and peace eternal. The conditioned mind is the source of sorrow; and the unconditioned mind is a non-actor and attains to the Supreme State of enlightenment. Hence one should work to remove all mental conditioning. That is known as contemplation or samadhi in which all the desires and hopes concerning the world have ceased and which is free from sorrow, fear and desire, and by which the Self rests in itself."

"That is known as the state of samadhi in which there is eternal satisfaction, clear perception of what is, egolessness, not being subject to the pairs of opposites, freedom from anxiety and from the wish to acquire or to reject."

"Liberation is but a synonym for a pure mind, correct Self-knowledge and a truly awakened state. The complete absence of all desires and hopes is liberation."

"The awakening or the enlightenment happens by itself, just like the sun's brilliance at noon. All cravings and desires come to an end in the awakened person; therefore, nirvana (liberation) arises in one without their desiring it. One is forever engaged in meditation; one is always established in one's own real nature: therefore, one does not seek anything or reject anything. Like a lamp in whose light all actions take place and in which the lamp itself is not interested, one lives and acts but is free from volition."

"One is a Mahakarta (great doer of actions) who is freed of doubts and performs appropriate actions in natural situations whether they be regarded as dharma (right) or adharma (wrong), without being swayed by likes and dislikes, by success and failure, without ego-sense or jealousy, remaining with one's mind in a state of silence and purity. They are unattached to anything but remain as a witness of everything, without selfish desires or motives, without excitement or exultation but with a mind at peace, without sorrow or grief, indifferent to action and inaction, whose very nature is peace and equilibrium or equanimity which is sustained in all situations."

"One is a Mahabhoktr (great enjoyer) who does not hate anything nor long for anything but enjoys all natural experiences, who does not cling to nor renounce anything even while engaged in actions, who does not experience

though experiencing, who witnesses the world play unaffected by it. Their Heart is not affected by pleasure and pain that arise in the course of life and the changes that cause confusion, and they regard with delight old age and death, sovereignty and poverty and even great calamities and fortunes. Their very nature is nonviolent and virtuous, and they enjoy what is sweet and what is bitter with equal relish, without making an arbitrary distinction 'This is enjoyable' and 'This is not'."

"One is a Mahatyagi (great renouncer) who has banished from his mind concepts like dharma and adharma, pain and pleasure, birth and death, all desires, all doubts, all convictions, who sees the falsity in the experience of pain by their body, mind, etc., who has realized 'I have no body, no birth, no right and no wrong', who has completely abandoned from their Heart the notion of world appearance."

"The Sage who has realized the truth and who is liberated from error here and now beholds this world as they would in deep sleep, without the least craving. They do not apprehend with their inner intelligence even those objects and experiences which seek them unsought: for their own Heart is withdrawn into itself. They have no hope for the future and they do not recall the past, nor do they even live in the present; and yet they do all. Asleep, they are awake; awake, they sleep. They do all, yet they do nothing. Inwardly having renounced everything though outwardly they appear to be busy, they are ever in a state of equilibrium. Their actions are entirely non-volitional."

"Only when it is realized that there is no creation at all, does real Self-knowledge arise which leads to liberation. Such liberation is unending, infinite and unconditioned. In it, one remains firmly rooted in Self-knowledge, without the least agitation. It is also known as eternal sleep, turiya, nirvana and moksha."

"Regard all actions everywhere as pure consciousness and live with your vision introverted. In sorrow and in calamity, in dire distress and in pain, remain free from sorrow within yourself, but behave as if in sorrow in accordance with propriety and in accordance with local etiquette, even shedding tears and wailing and seemingly experiencing pleasure and pain. While enjoying the company of your wife and participating in festivals, etc., manifest delight as if you were subject to mental conditioning. With your gaze turned inward, swimming in the bliss of the Self and with your heart and mind at peace, what you do you do not do. Lead an active life though remaining inwardly as if in the deep sleep state."

Oneness

"While remaining active in this world be without the mind and realize that you are pure Consciousness. Abandon notions such as 'This is mine', 'That is he', 'This I am' and be established in the Consciousness of undivided Oneness. As long as the body lasts, consider the present and the future with an equanimous consciousness. Abandon the impurity of objective perception, hopes, and desires: remain established in Self-knowledge. Give up notions of auspicious and inauspicious happenings, give up visions of the desirable and undesirable: know that you are the essence of Consciousness. Realize that subject, object and actions do not touch you: remain as pure Consciousness without any disturbance in it. Know 'I am the all' and live in the waking state as if in deep sleep. Be freed from conditions known as duality and non-duality: and remain in a state of equilibrium which is a state of pure Consciousness and freedom. Realize that this Cosmic Consciousness is indivisible into 'I' and 'the other'; thus remain firm and unshakable."

"The omnipresent, infinite Self can never be bound; so how is it to be liberated?"

"You are the eternal infinite light, pure and extremely subtle."

"It is only when the division between the seer and the seen is given up, only when the two are 'seen' as of one substance, that the truth is realized."

"The Lord can be realized only if one is firmly established in the unreality of the universe even as the blueness of the sky is unreal. Dualism presupposes unity, and non-dualism suggests dualism. Only when the creation is known to be utterly nonexistent is the Lord (the Supreme Self) realized."

"Abandon all notion of division. Rest in Self-knowledge with your awareness extending just a little outside. Thus, by the practice of Self-awareness which is beginning-less and endless, you will gradually reach that Supreme state of Consciousness in which there is no duality and which is beyond all materiality. In it, there is neither unity nor diversity but Supreme peace."

"The mind is liberated by the firm conviction that everything is the Supreme Self. Ideas and thoughts are bondage; and their coming to an end is liberation. Therefore, be free of them and do whatever has to be done spontaneously."

"I do not let hopes and expectations touch me and even when a thing is old and worn out I look upon it with fresh eyes as if it were new. I rejoice with the happy ones and share the grief of the grief stricken, for I am the friend of all, knowing I belong to none and none belongs to me. I know that I am the world, all the activities in it and its intelligence. I know that everything

at all times, everywhere, is but the One Cosmic Consciousness."

"In the scriptures, words have been used in order to facilitate the imparting of instruction. Cause and effect, the Self and the Lord, difference and non-difference, knowledge and ignorance, pain and pleasure—all these pairs have been invented for the instruction of the ignorant. They are not real in themselves. All this discussion and argumentation take place only in and because of ignorance; when there is Knowledge there is no duality. When the truth is known, all descriptions cease, and silence alone remains."

"In the infinite Self, there is no creator, no creation, no worlds, no heaven, no humans, no demons, no bodies, no elements, no time, no existence and no destruction, no 'you', no 'I', no self, no that, no truth, no falsehood (none of these), no notion of diversity, no contemplation and no enjoyment. Whatever is, is that Supreme peace. There is no beginning, no middle and no end: all is all at all times, beyond the comprehension of the mind and the speech."

"Pure meditation is perfect awakening or enlightenment. The realization that the objective universe does not exist is perfect awakening. It does not resemble a state of inertia, nor deep sleep, nor is it an unreal imaginary state. In it, the universe exists as it is but it is dissolved at the same time. In it, there are no concepts of unity, diversity, their mixture and their nonexistence. In it, there is Supreme peace."

"It is beyond description. At the end of the investigation utter silence alone remains."

"This Self dwells in all bodies even as fragrance resides in flowers. It is not realized by all because no one enquires into the truth concerning the Self. If it is realized through self-enquiry, there is an instant experience of Supreme Bliss and one gets an undying vision of the truth; all fetters drop away, all enemies are quelled and cravings do not agitate the mind. When it is seen, everything is seen; when it is heard, everything is heard; when it is touched, everything is touched—for the world is because it is."

"There is naught known as 'real', 'unreal', 'experiencer' nor 'experience', nor are these experienced. Whatever is, is indescribable. In the infinite Consciousness all distinctions between 'being' and 'nonbeing' vanish. Brahman (the Supreme Self) exists as Brahman in Brahman, just as space exists as space in space. That which is known as creation is the indivisible Brahman only. In the vision of the knowers of reality, all that exists is pure void. I am void, you are void, the universe is pure void. This Supreme truth is established only in total silence, not by logic, discussion and argumentation."

Om Asatoma Sat Gamaya
Tamasoma Jyotir Gamaya
Mrityorma Amritam Gamaya

Om Lokah Samasta Sukhino Bhavantu
Om Shantih Shantih Shantihi

Lead us from Untruth to Truth
Lead us from the Darkness of Ignorance
to the Light of Knowledge
Lead us from Death to Eternity

May all Beings Everywhere be Happy and at Peace
May there be Only Peace

www.ingramcontent.com/pod-product-compliance
Lightning Source LLC
Chambersburg PA
CBHW030828060726
47590CB00004B/1451